CONSERVATORY CANADA™

New Millennium Piano Series
GRADE 1

Repertoire List Pieces and Studies of Conservatory Canada - Grade 1

T0057169

© 1999 Conservatory Canada
Published and Distributed by Novus Via Music Group Inc.
Edition updated May 2016
All Rights Reserved

ISBN 978-0-88909-212-9

The intellectual property in this book is protected under international copyright treaties. Copyright exists to encourage and support the work of creators in society.
Please respect the creators of this publication and the intent of copyright law and do not photocopy from this book.
Reproduction of any part of this book without the permission of the publisher may lead to prosecution.

Novus Via Music Group Inc.
189 Douglas Street, Stratford, Ontario, Canada N5A 5P8
(519) 273-7520 www.NVmusicgroup.com

cover design:
Robin E. Cook, AOCA

About the Series

The *New Millennium Piano Series* is the official repertoire books for CONSERVATORY CANADA™ examinations. This graded series, in eleven volumes (Pre-Grade 1 to Grade 10), is designed not only to serve the needs of students, teachers and parents for examinations, but it is also a valuable teaching resource and comprehensive anthology for any pianist. The list pieces have been carefully selected and edited, and represent repertoire from the Baroque, Classical, Romantic/Impressionist and 20th century periods. For your convenience, we have included the list pieces AND studies for each grade in one volume. In choosing the studies, we have not only considered their suitability in building technique, but we have also tried to ensure that they could stand as recital repertoire in their own right. In addition, each volume also includes a graded arrangement of *O Canada* (with words in English and French). Volumes for grades 1 to 8 include a glossary containing a short biography of each composer represented in the volume. CONSERVATORY CANADA™ encourages at least one Canadian composition be performed in every examination. Composers working in Canada are well represented in the series. A small asterisk next to their name identifies them.

Notes on Editing

Most composers in the Baroque and Classical periods included only sparse dynamic, articulation, tempo and other performance indications in their scores. Where we felt it necessary, we have added suggested markings. Whenever possible, ornaments have been realized using the latest scholarship as guidelines. For the works of J.S. Bach, students are urged to consult Bach's own table of ornaments as given in the volumes for grades 7 to 10. The *New Millennium Piano Series* is not an Urtext edition. All editorial markings, along with fingering and pedaling, are intended to be helpful suggestions rather than a final authority. The choice of tempo is a matter of personal taste, technical ability, and appropriateness of style. Most of our suggested metronome markings are expressed within a range of tempi. In the 19th and 20th centuries, composers of piano music included more performance indications in their scores, and as a consequence, fewer editorial markings have been required.

Slurs are used to indicate legato notes and do not necessarily indicate a phrase. In accordance with Conservatory Canada's policy regarding redundant accidentals, we have followed the practice that a barline cancels an accidental. Unnecessary accidentals following the barline have been used only in exceptional circumstances.

Bearing in mind acceptable performance practices, you are free to use your own judgement and imagination in changing any editorial markings, especially in the areas of dynamics, articulation, fingering, and the discretionary use of pedal.

The pieces in the *New Millennium Piano Series* have been chosen as an introduction to enjoyable repertoire that is fun to play, while at the same time, helps to develop your technique and musicianship. We hope you will explore the broad variety of styles and periods represented in this series. We suggest that you also explore as many pieces and studies as possible before deciding which ones you will perform in an examination or musical evaluation.

Fingering Suggestions

In an effort to acknowledge the exploration of creative fingering possibilities, alternate fingering suggestions are given in parentheses on the score for your consideration. CONSERVATORY CANADA™ encourages investigation of different fingering possibilities in order to reveal those that are best suited to the individual pianist's hands.

The Conservatory Canada Piano Syllabus gives full details regarding examinations. Students, teachers and parents are advised to consult the most recent syllabus online for current requirements, regulations, procedures and deadlines for application.
www.conservatorycanada.ca

TABLE OF CONTENTS

*indicates Canadian composer

Allemande in G

Johann Hermann Schein
(1586–1630)

Allegro ♩ = 126–144

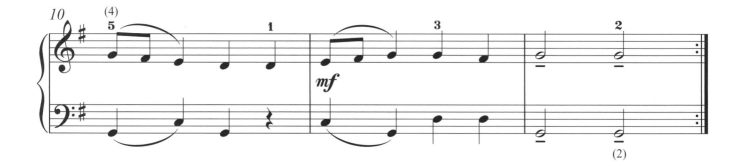

Non-slurred quarter notes in the left hand may be played detached.

Menuet in D Minor

Jean-Baptiste Lully
(1632–1687)

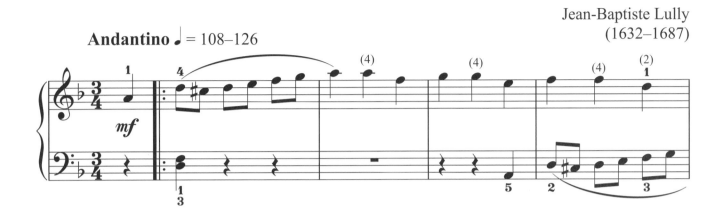

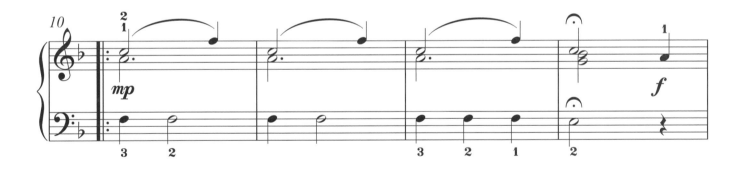

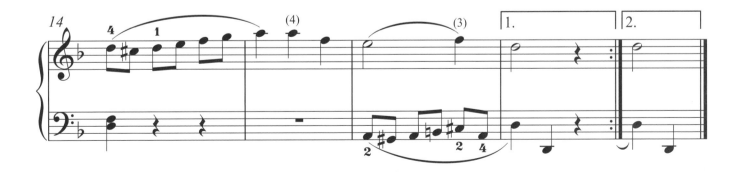

Non-slurred quarter notes may be played detached.

List A

Bourrée

from *Partita in B Minor for Violin*, BWV 1002

Johann Sebastian Bach
(1685–1750)

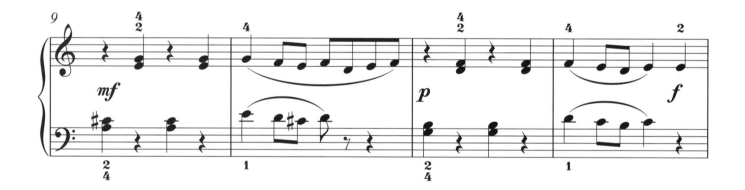

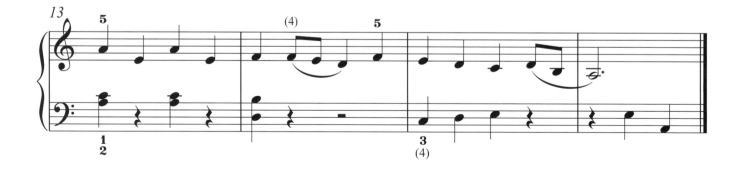

Non-slurred quarter notes in the left hand may be played detached.

List A

Minuet in F

Jean-Henri D'Anglebert
(1635–1691)

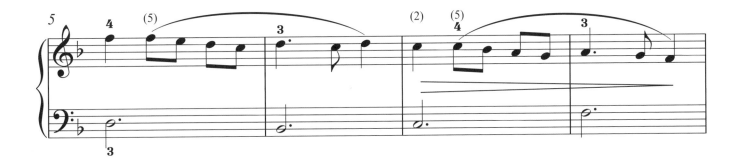

Non-slurred quarter notes may be played detached.

Minuet in D Minor

Johann Krieger
(1651–1735)

Moderato espressivo ♩ = 108–120

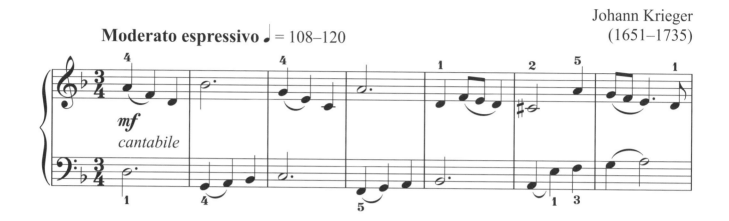

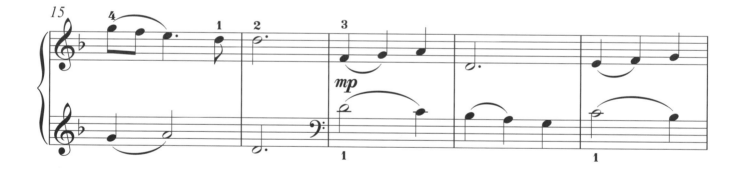

Non-slurred quarter notes in the left hand may be played detached.

List A

Air in D Minor

Henry Purcell
(1659–1695)

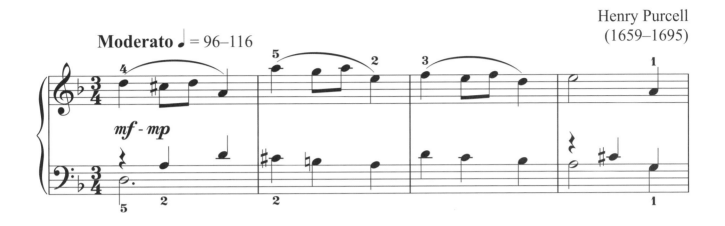

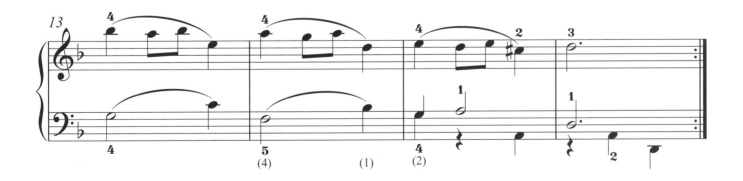

Non-slurred quarter notes may be played detached.

List A

Chorale

Schaffs mit Mir, BWV 514

Johann Sebastian Bach
(1685–1750)

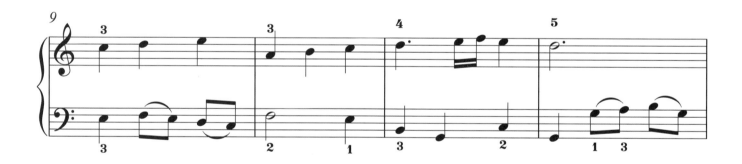

Non-slurred quarter notes in the left hand may be played detached.

List A

A Trumpet Minuet

Jeremiah Clarke
(c1674–1707)

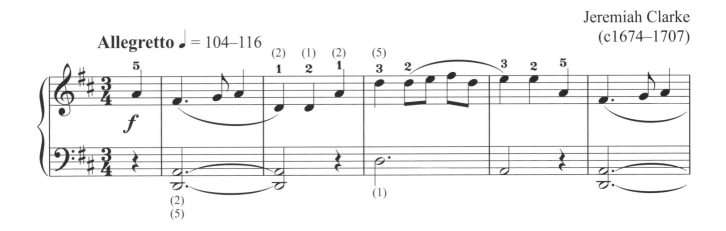

Non-slurred quarter notes may be played detached.

Fantasia in B Flat

Georg Philipp Telemann
(1681–1767)

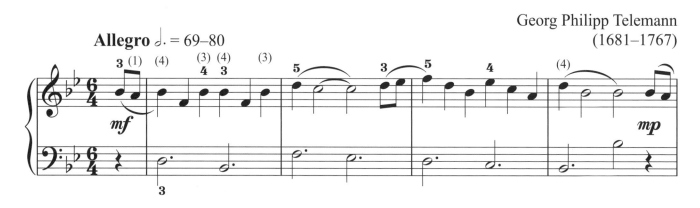
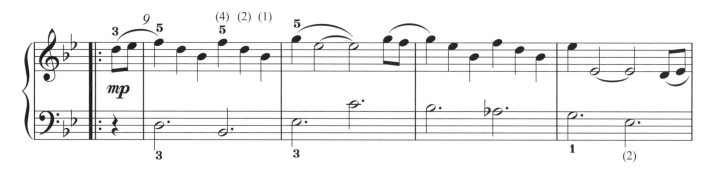

Non-slurred quarter notes may be played detached.

List A

The Two Parrots

Johann Philipp Kirnberger
(1721–1783)

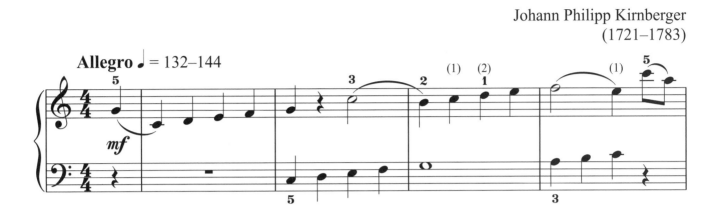

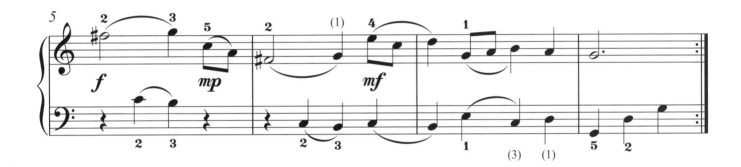

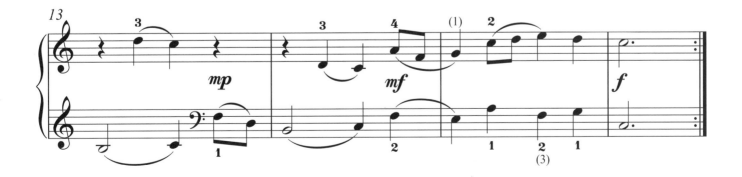

Non-slurred quarter notes may be played detached.

Menuet in G Minor

BWV 822

Johann Sebastian Bach
(1685–1750)

Andante ♩ = 88–104

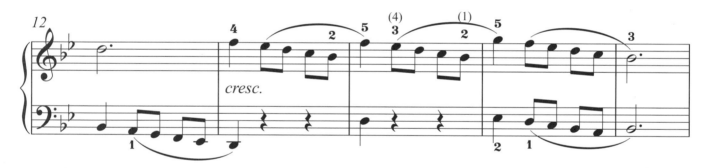

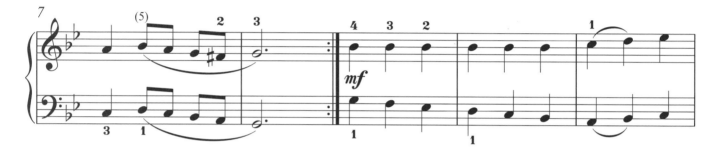

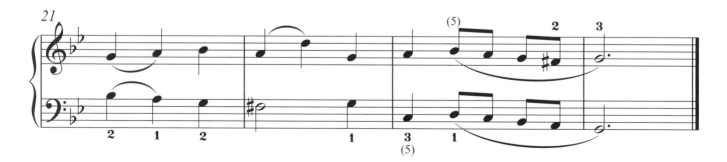

Non-slurred quarter notes may be played detached.

List B

Menuet in C

Hob. IX:29

Franz Joseph Haydn
(1732–1809)

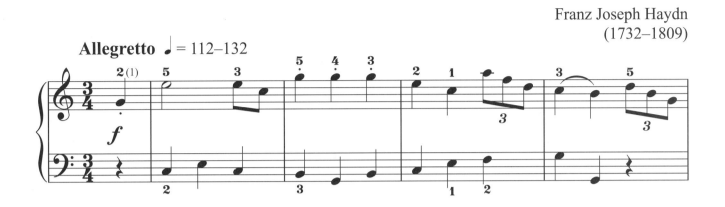

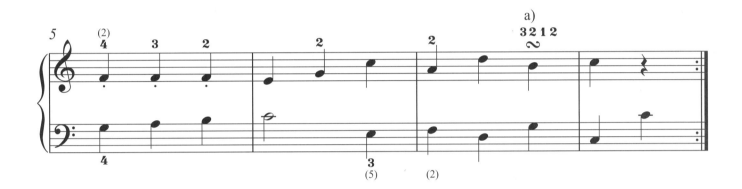

a) Ornament.
Left hand quarter notes may be played detached.

Sonatina
Op. 36, No. 3 (2nd movement)

Muzio Clementi
(1752–1832)

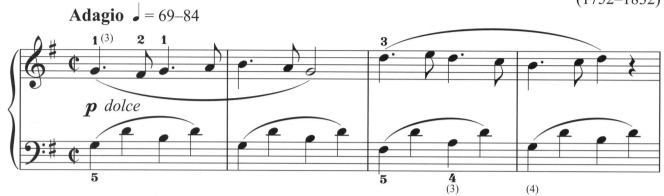

a) Grace notes to be played on the beat.

Evening Song

Daniel Gottlob Türk
(1756–1813)

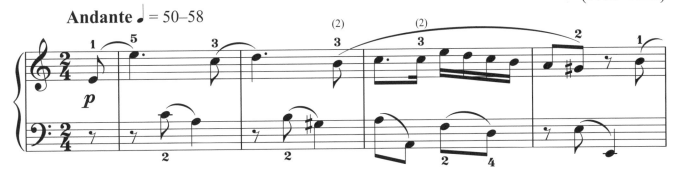

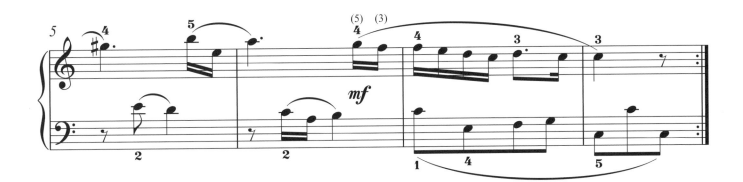

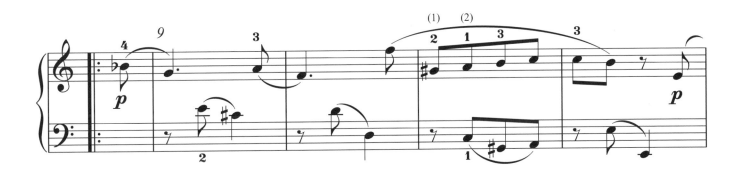

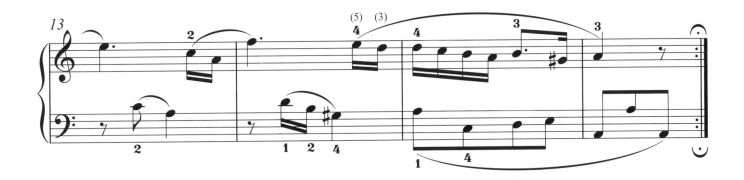

Minuet in C

K 6

Wolfgang Amadeus Mozart
(1756–1791)

Moderato ♩ = 100–116

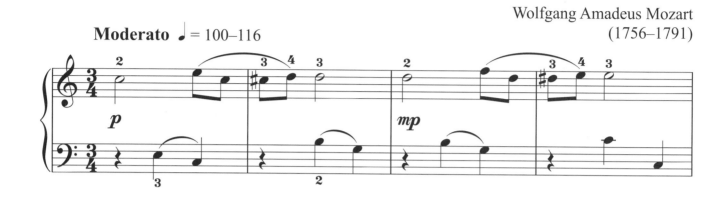

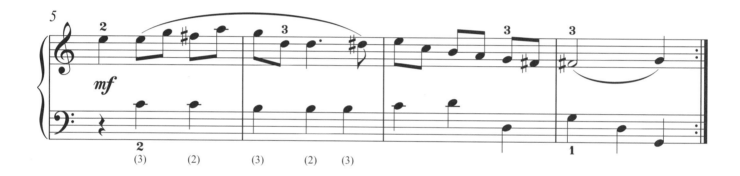

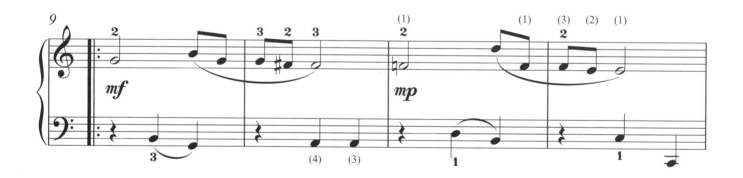

List B

Russian Folk Song

theme from *Variations for Violin and Piano*, Op. 107, No. 3

Ludwig van Beethoven
(1770–1827)

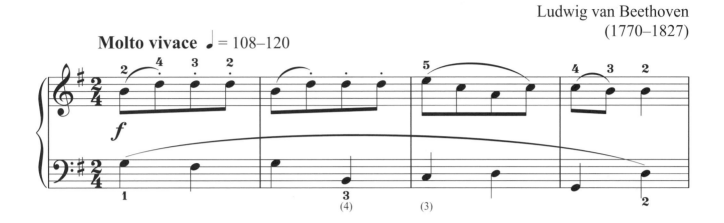

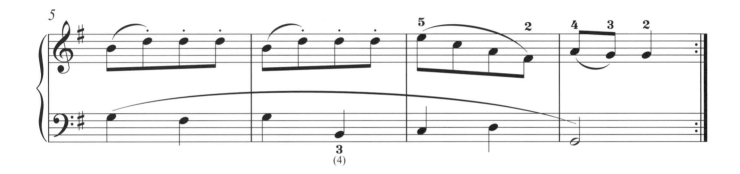

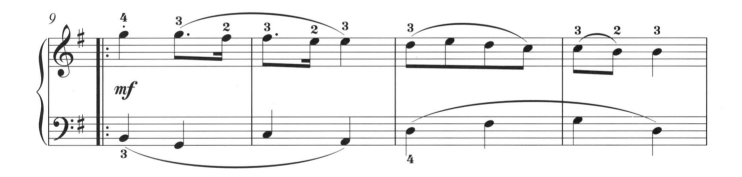

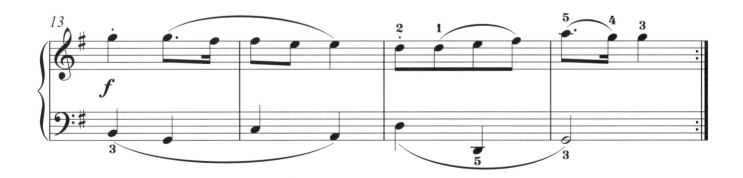

Ecossaise in G

Carl Maria von Weber
(1786–1826)

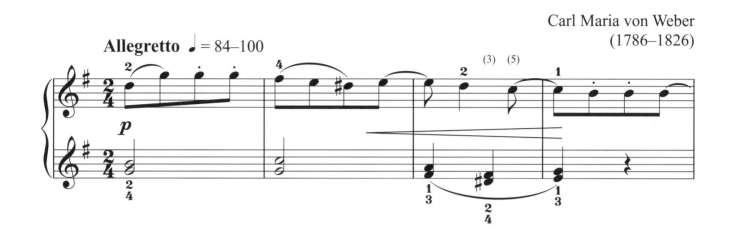

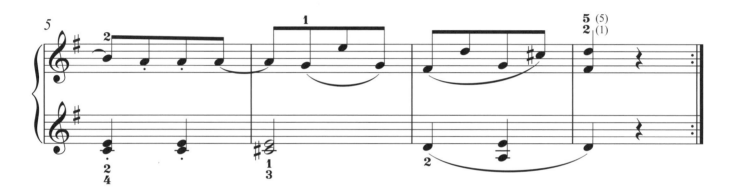

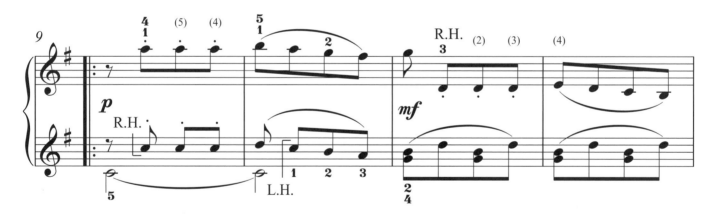

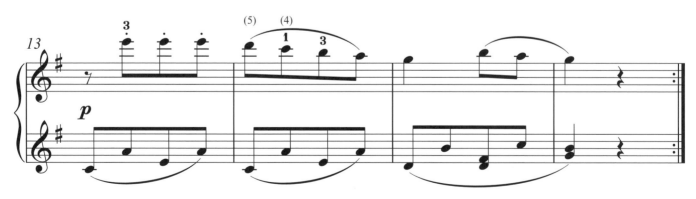

List B

Minuet in E

Franz Joseph Haydn
(1732–1809)

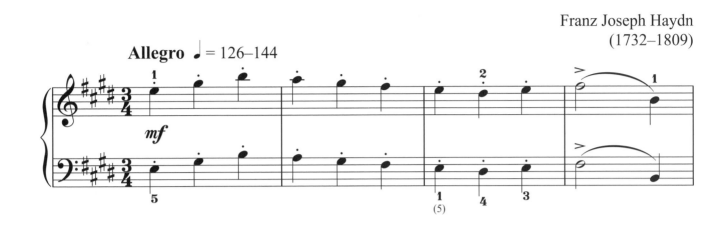

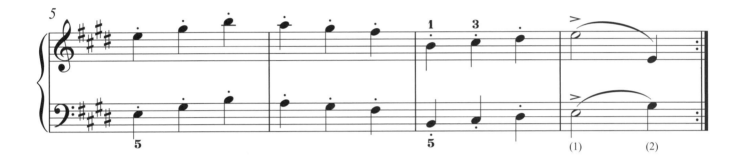

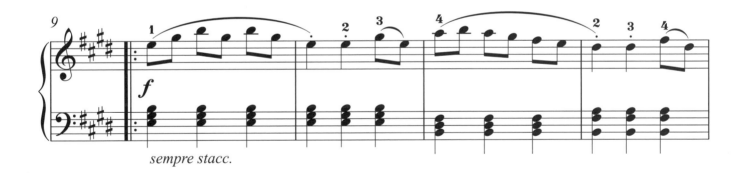

Sonatina in C

Jacob Schmitt
(1803–1853)

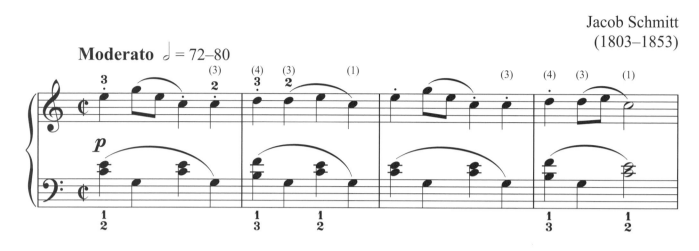

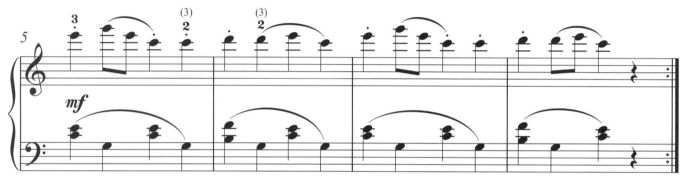

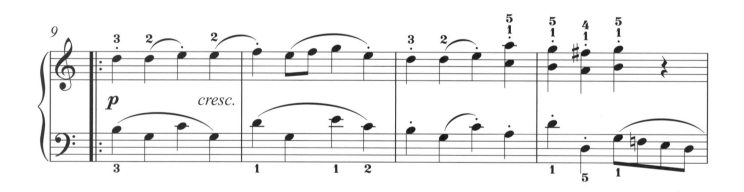

Ecossaise in G

Franz Peter Schubert
(1797-1828)

Allegretto ♩ = 126–144

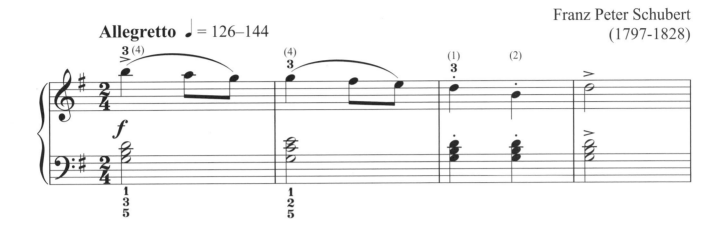

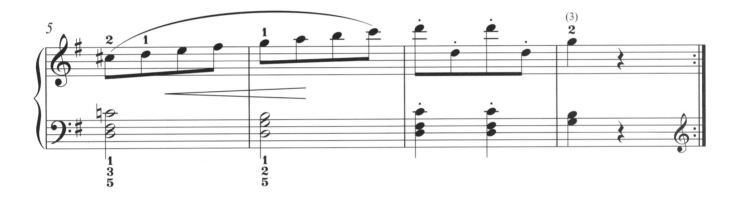

List B

The Hunt

Cornelius Gurlitt
(1820–1901)

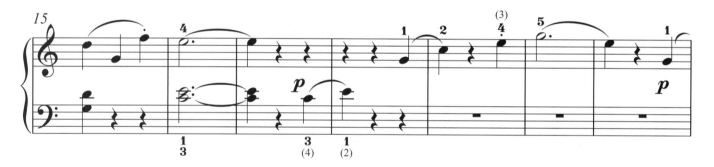

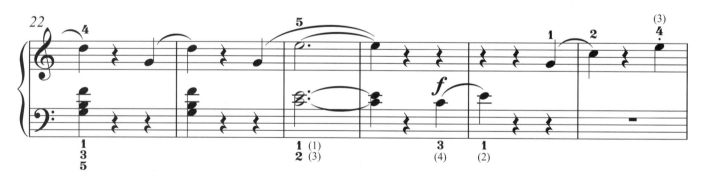

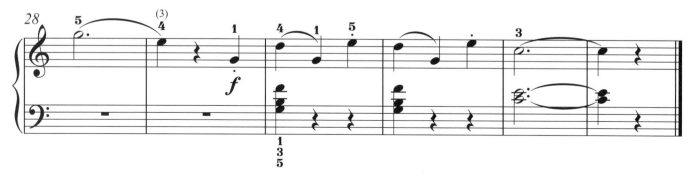

List B

Sonatina in C

(1st movement)

William Duncombe
(fl. 1760-1790)

The Prowling Pussy Cat

William Gillock
(1917–1993)

Stealthily ♩ = 104–112

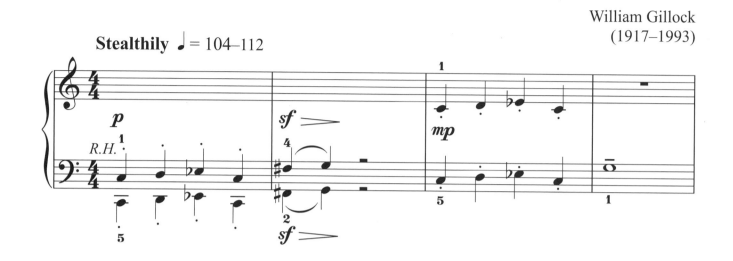

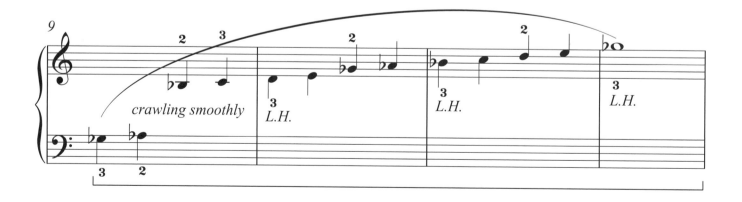

© 1964, Charles Scribner's Sons—© Assigned 1966 to The Willis Music Co. Used by permission.

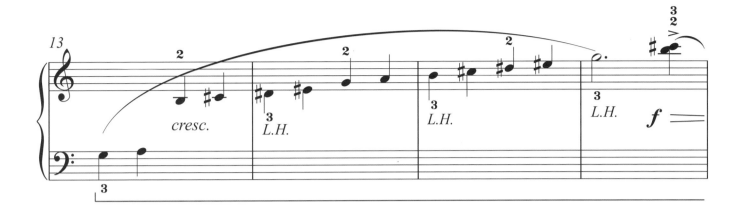

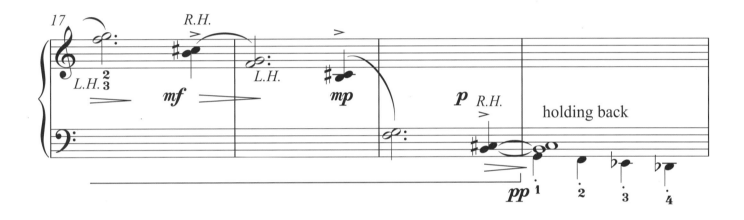

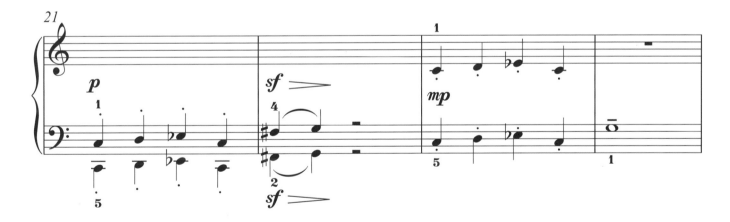

Waterlilies

Christopher Norton
(1953-   )

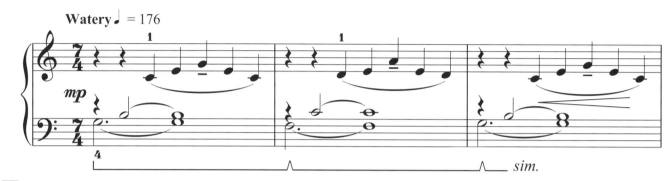

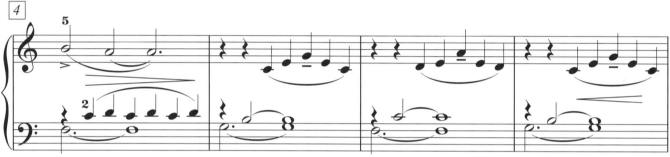

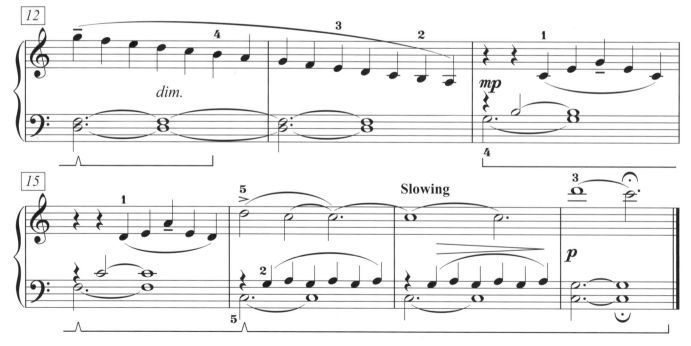

© Novus Via Music Group, Inc.; from *American Popular Piano Level 3 Etudes*, 2006.
Used with permission of the publisher.

List C

Barkey's Boogie

*Donald F. Cook
(1937–   )

With energy ♩ = 126–138

© D.F. Cook. Used by permission.

Wallabies Waltzing

Ruth Perdew
(20th century)

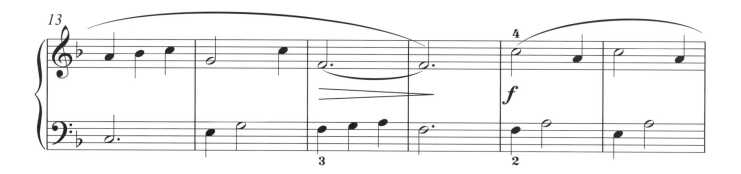

© Myklas Music Press. Used by permission.

List C

Spider Blues

Christopher Norton
(1953-   )

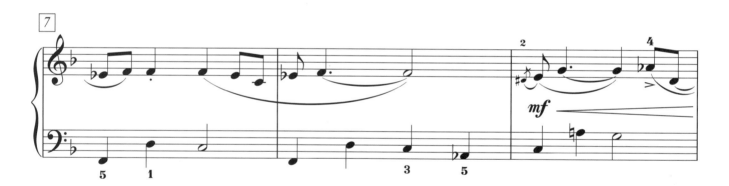

© Novus Via Music Group, Inc.; from *American Popular Piano Level 3 Repertoire*, 2006.
Used with permission of the publisher.

List C

Citadel Hill

Canadian Folk Song
adapted from *Fowke/Johnston

Happily

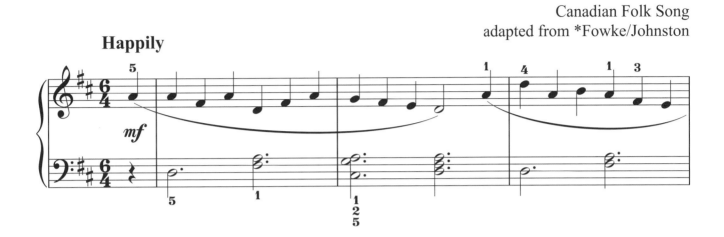

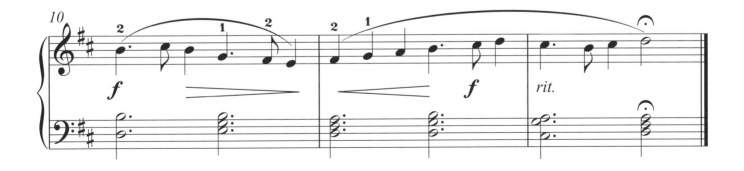

© 2008 Debra Wanless.
Used by permission of the arranger.

List C

Stairway

from *Microjazz for Starters*

Christopher Norton
(1953–   )

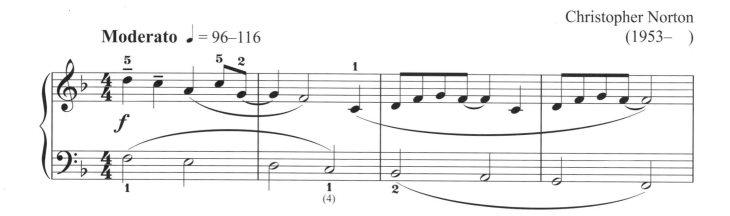

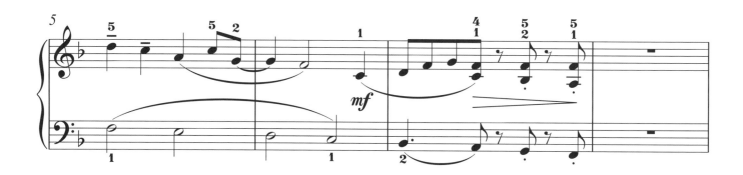

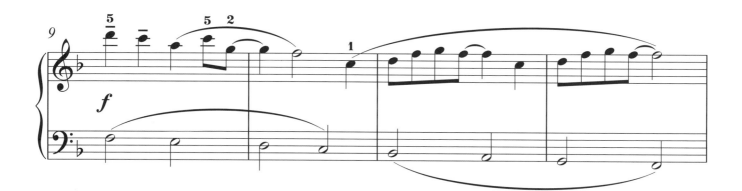

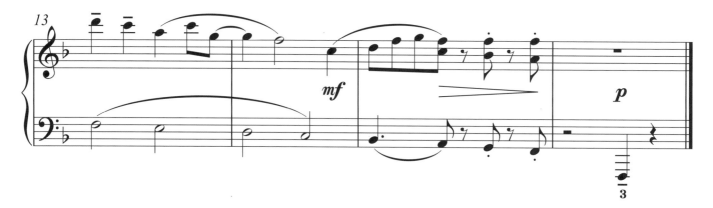

© 1986, Boosey & Hawkes Music Publishing Ltd. Reprinted by permission of Boosey & Hawkes Inc.

This page intentionally left blank
to facilitate page turns.

Thumbelina

from *Sketches from Hans Christian Anderson*

Yvonne Adair
(1897–1990)

Light and dainty ♩ = 120–138

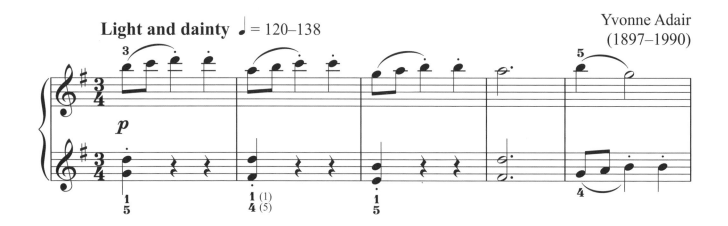

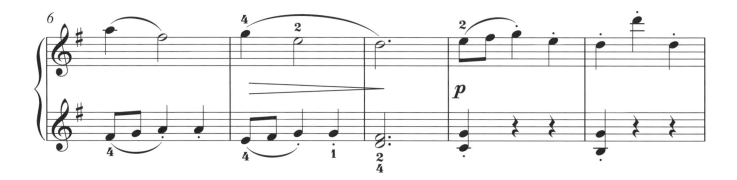

© 1931, Oxford University Press. Reprinted by permission.

List C

Waltz in A Minor

Dmitri Shostakovich
(1906–1975)

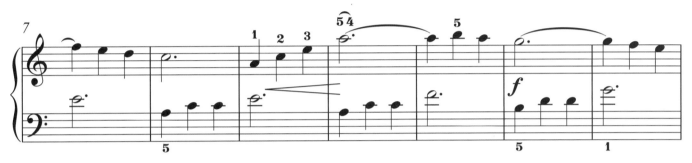

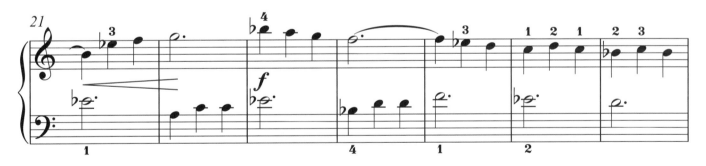

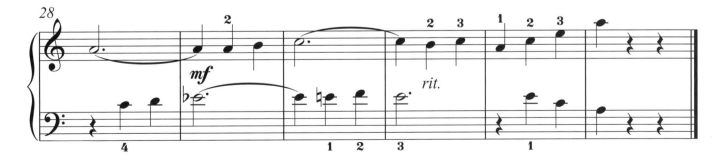

© G. Schirmer. Used by permission.

Children's Song

from *For Children*, Vol. 1, No. 3

Béla Bartók
(1881–1945)

Study

A Little Joke

Op. 39, No. 12

Dmitry Borisovich Kabalevsky
(1904–1987)

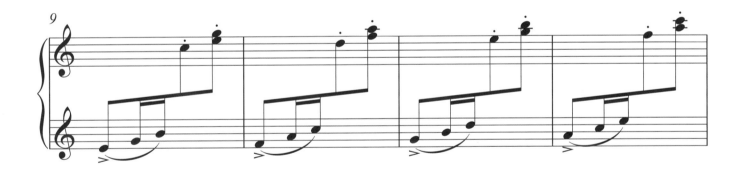

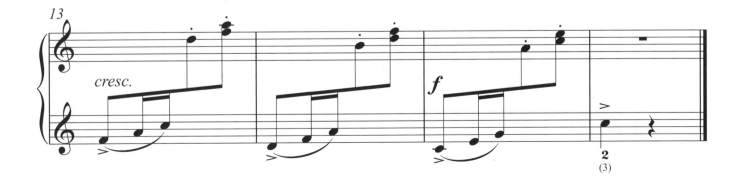

© Alfred Publishing Co. Used by permission.

Study

Daytime Dreaming

Christopher Norton
(1953-   )

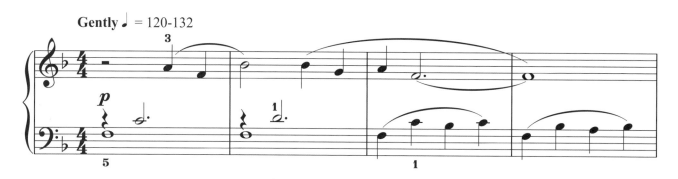

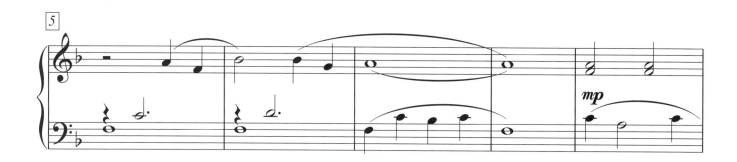

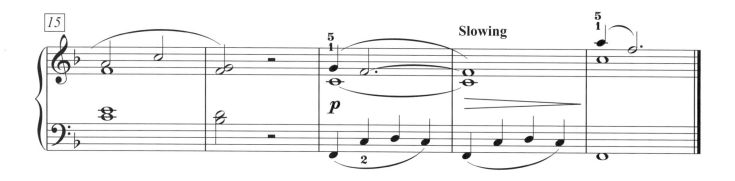

© Novus Via Music Group, Inc.; from *American Popular Piano Level 2 Etudes*, 2006.
Used with permission of the publisher.

Study

Twice As Fast, Half As Slow

from *Six Mobiles*, Vol. 1

*John Beckwith
(1927–   )

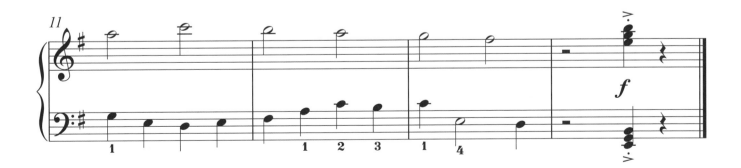

© Berandol. Used by permission.

42

Amusement

*Maya Badian
(1945–   )

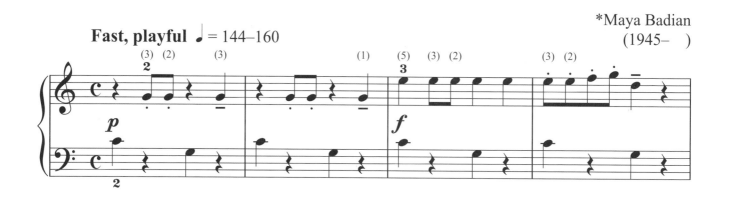

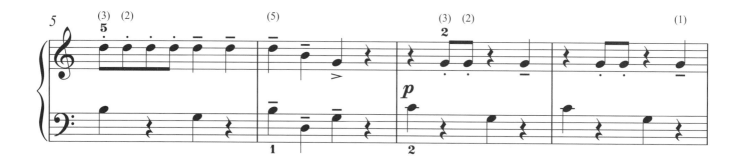

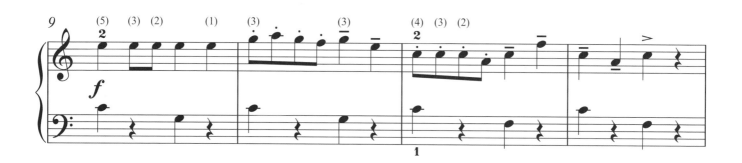

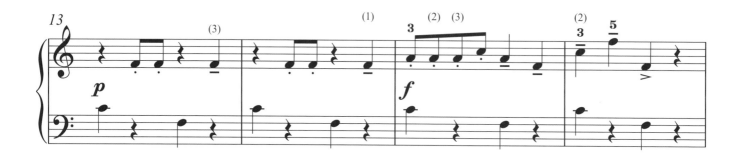

© Maya Badian. Used by permission.

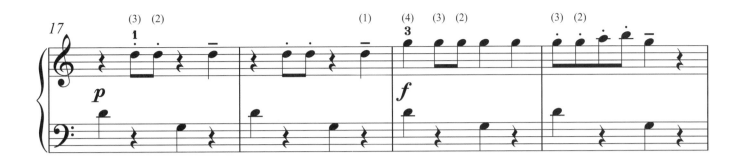

Drifting Clouds

Jon Paul George
(1944–1982)

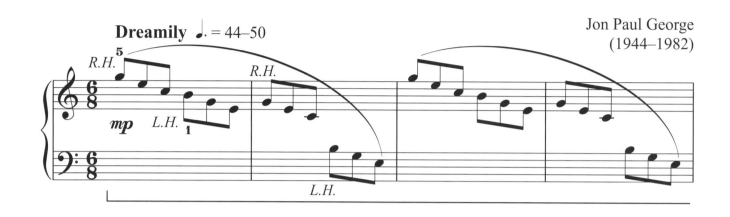

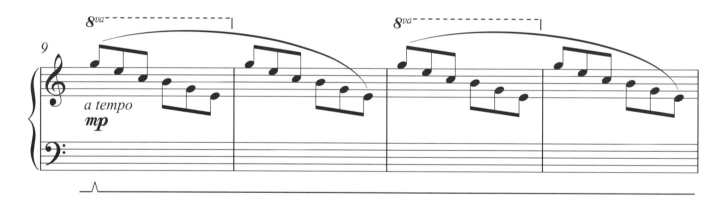

© 1969, Summy-Birchard Music, a division of Summy Birchard Inc. Copyright renewed. All rights reserved. Used by permission.

Study

Thirds

Antony Hopkins
(1921–   )

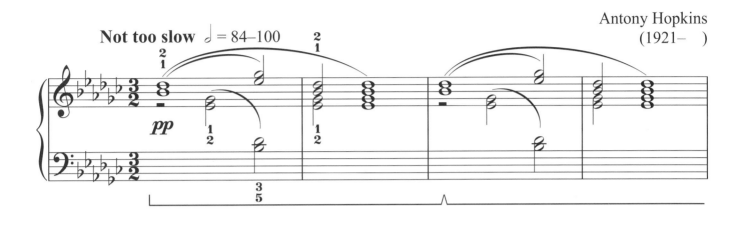

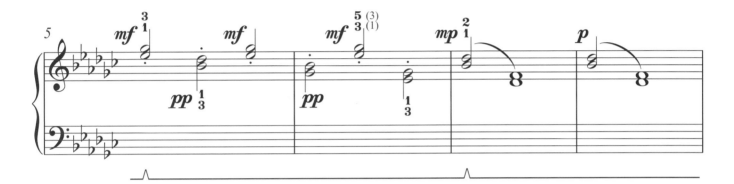

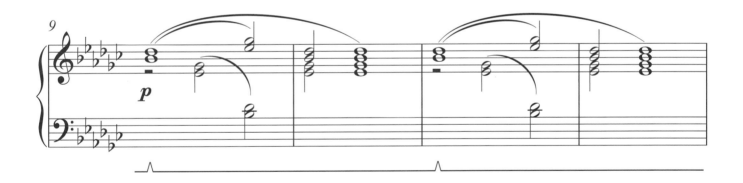

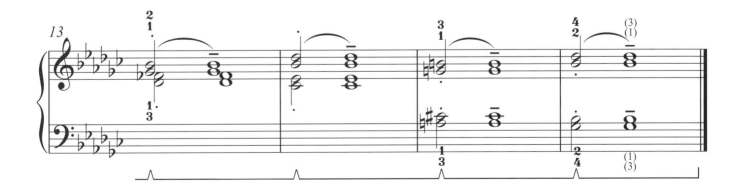

© Dr. Antony Hopkins. Used by permission.

Chromatic Rag

*Beverly Porter
(1930–)

© Beverly Porter. Used by permission.

Study

Snake Charmer

Jon Paul George
(1944–1982)

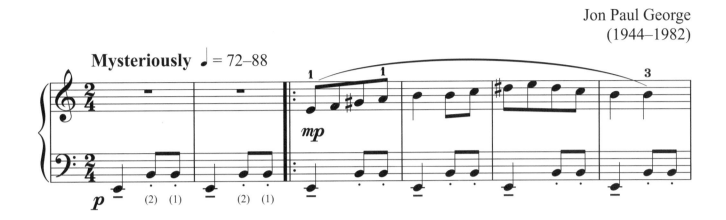

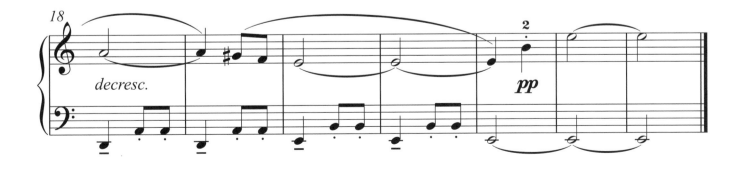

© 1970, Summy-Birchard Music, a division of Summy Birchard Inc. Copyright renewed. All rights reserved. Used by permission.

O Canada

Written in French by Adophe-Basile Routhier (1839-1920) in Quebec City and first performed there in 1880 to a musical setting by Calixa Lavallée. Translated into English in 1908 by Robert Stanley Weir (1858-1926). Approved as Canada's national anthem by the Parliament of Canada in 1967 and officially adopted in 1980.

*Calixa Lavallée
(1842–1891)
*arr. D.F. Cook

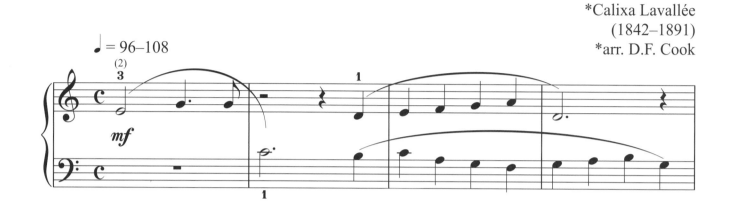

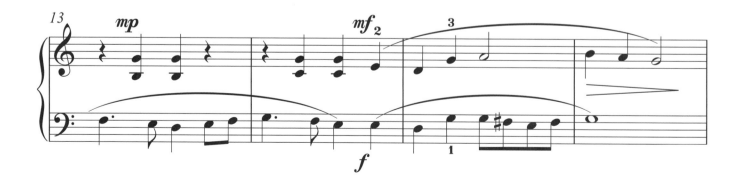

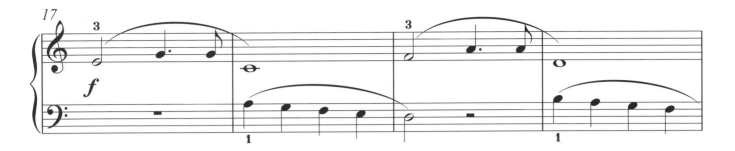

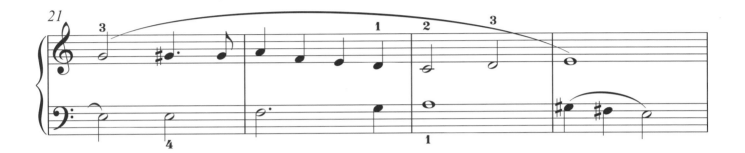

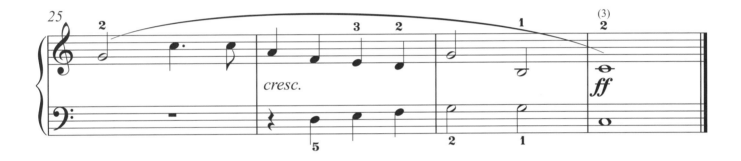

Ô Canada! Terre de nos aïeux,	O Canada! Our home and native land!
Ton front est ceint de fleurons glorieux!	True patriot love in all of us command.
Car ton bras sait porter l'épée,	With glowing hearts we see thee rise,
Il sait porter la croix!	The True North strong and free!
Ton histoire est une épopée	From far and wide,
Des plus brillants exploits.	O Canada, we stand on guard for thee.
Et ta valeur, de foi trempée,	God keep our land glorious and free!
Protégera nos foyers et nos droits.	O Canada, we stand on guard for thee.
Protégera nos foyers et nos droits.	O Canada, we stand on guard for thee.

Glossary of Composers

About The Composers In Grade One

Students are encouraged to explore online resources to expand their individual knowledge of the composers listed.

ADAIR, Yvonne (20th century). BRITAIN. Little is known about Adair except that she composes instructional piano music. Her children's collections include *Sketches for Hans Christian Anderson* and *Little Dog Tales*.

BACH, Johann Sebastian (1685-1750). GERMANY. Bach was born into a family that had been musicians for nearly 200 years. Bach's first teacher was his father. He died when Bach was only ten, so Bach went to live and study with his older brother. Throughout his life, Bach worked as an organist, violinist, teacher and composer. He married twice and had 20 children, ten of whom died in infancy. Four of his sons became famous musicians. During his lifetime, Bach was famous as an organist, but we remember him today as a composer of music for church, orchestra, choir, organ and keyboard. His *Anna Magdalena's Notebook* was a gift he gave his second wife on her 24th birthday. It's filled with family favourites, ideal for the young pianist.

*BADIAN, Maya (born 1945). CANADA. Born in Romania, Dr. Maya Badian received her formal musical training at the Bucharest Conservatory and continued her studies in Italy, Germany and Canada. She became a Canadian citizen in 1990 and now lives in Ottawa, Ontario. She has composed more than 600 pieces for soloists, chamber ensemble, orchestra, and keyboard, many of which have been featured around the world.

BARTÓK, Béla (1881-1945). HUNGARY. Bartók was a composer and pianist. He studied piano with his mother and gave his first concert when he was only ten years old. Bartók was extremely interested in folk music and spent a great deal of time collecting Hungarian and Slovakian folk music. Though he emigrated to New York City, U.S.A. in 1940, he continued to base many of his compositions on the folk music of his homeland. His *For Children, Vol I* is based on Hungarian folk tunes.

*BECKWITH, John (born 1927). CANADA. Born in Victoria, British Columbia, Beckwith grew up with musical parents who encouraged his talent. He studied in Toronto with Alberto Guerrero, and later in France with Nadia Boulanger. Dr. Beckwith makes his home in Toronto, where he works as a composer, writer, educator,

pianist and broadcaster. He has composed opera, chamber music, choral and piano music.

BEETHOVEN, Ludwig van (1770-1827). GERMANY. Beethoven had a great influence upon the development of music from the Classical style to the Romantic. His life was difficult, but even his deafness in later life did not stop him from composing. His nine symphonies changed orchestral music forever, and his piano works are considered among the most important repertoire ever composed for that instrument. Most of Beethoven's music is intended for experienced performers; however the Russian Folk Song in this book will give young pianists an introduction to his style.

*CHATMAN, Stephen (born 1950). CANADA. Born in the United States, Chatman currently teaches composition at the University of British Columbia. His compositions have won many awards, and include works for orchestra, instrumental solos and ensembles, and piano.

CLARKE, Jeremiah (c1674-1707). BRITAIN. Clarke was a composer and organist who studied with John Blow at the Chapel Royal. Clarke held organist posts at Westminster Abbey, St. Paul's Cathedral and the Chapel Royal. He is most famous for his anthems and odes for choir, although he composed some keyboard music. Today, his famous *Trumpet Voluntary* is a popular piece at weddings.

CLEMENTI, Muzio (1752-1832). BRITAIN. Born in Rome, Italy, Clementi displayed such unusual musical talent that at the early age of 14 he was sent to England to continue his studies. He soon became the toast of London as a concert pianist and composer. Though he travelled extensively throughout Europe giving concerts, he made London his home where he earned a reputation as a successful composer, conductor, teacher, pianist, music publisher and piano manufacturer. Clementi was one of the first to compose pieces for the then new pianoforte, and composed 64 piano sonatas. He knew Haydn, Mozart and Beethoven. Beethoven was particularly fond of Clementi's sonatas and was influenced by them.

*COOK, Donald F. (born 1937). CANADA. Cook grew up and received his early music training in St. John's, Newfoundland. After further studies in New York City and London, England, Dr. Cook returned to Newfoundland to become the founding director of the School of Music at Memorial University. Since 1992, he has served as Principal of Western Ontario Conservatory (now, CONSERVATORY CANADA™).

D'ANGELBERT, Jean-Henri (1635-1691). FRANCE. Angelbert was a harpsichordist, organist and composer who served in the court of the Duc d'Orleans and also for Henry XIV. His most famous work is probably *Pieces de Clavessin* which includes original compositions and transcriptions of works by the famous French opera composer, Jean-Baptiste Lully.

DUNCOMBE, William (fl. 1760-1790). BRITAIN. Duncombe wa a composer, harpsichordist and pianist during the latter part of the eighteenth century. He came from a well-known literary and musical family. His two-volume collection *Progressive Lessons for the Harpsichord and Pianoforte* was published in 1785.

GEORGE, Jon Paul (1944-1982). UNITED STATES. George was born in Illinois. He studied piano as a young boy and taught himself to play guitar as a teenager. In addition to composing piano solos and duets for young people, he operated a school of music in Orange City, Florida.

GILLOCK, William Lawson (1917-1993). UNITED STATES. Gillock was born on a small farm in Missouri. He had little opportunity to learn music while he was growing up and didn't have his first real music lesson until he was at university. He opened a private music studio in New Orleans and taught there for over 20 years. He eventually gave up private teaching and moved to Dallas, Texas to concentrate on composing music for young pianists, and working as a clinician and adjudicator.

GURLITT, Cornelius (1820-1901). GERMANY. Gurlitt was an organist, composer and teacher who wrote nearly 250 works. Today, he is best known for his piano music which is similar in style to Schumann's. These pleasant piano pieces often have descriptive titles such as *Morning Prayer*, *Grandfather's Birthday* and *The Music Box*.

*HANSEN, Joan (born 1941). CANADA. Born in Prince Albert, Saskatchewan, Hansen is a composer and teacher, and has received numerous awards for her compositions, including pieces for piano, violin, woodwind, and choir. She lives in Vancouver, British Columbia where she is a teacher, adjudicator and clinician specializing in 20th century music.

HAYDN, Franz Joseph (1732-1809). AUSTRIA. At the age of eight, Haydn was accepted as a chorister at St. Stephen's Cathedral in Vienna, where he received his early musical education. He spent most of his working life as music director and composer for Prince Esterhazy, during which time Haydn composed orchestra works, church music, chamber music, keyboard music and solo songs. He is considered to be the Father of the Symphony, and, because he lived to a ripe old age, was lovingly referred to as 'Papa Haydn'.

HOPKINS, Antony (born 1921). BRITAIN. A graduate of the Royal College of Music, Hopkins is a composer and pianist. His works include piano sonatas, chamber music, solo songs, stage music and music for films. He also wrote books on musical analysis and was a radio broadcaster.

KABALEVSKY, Dmitry Borisovich (1904-1987). RUSSIA. Kabalevsky studied and later taught at the Moscow Conservatory. He composed chamber music, orchestral and choral music, and operas. His piano music for children is delightfully rhythmic and often humourous.

KIRNBERGER, Johann Philipp (1721-1783). GERMANY. Kirnberger was a composer, violinist and teacher who studied with J.S. Bach in Leipzig, Germany. Kirnberger composed instrumental and vocal works, keyboard pieces, trio sonatas, and suites. He also published several works on piano technique.

KRIEGER, Johann (1651-1735). GERMANY. Krieger came from a family of musicians. He spent most of his life as music director and organist for the town of Zittau, Germany. He wrote motets, masses, harpsichord suites and organ music, though little of it was published in his lifetime. Händel admired Krieger's organ preludes and fugues.

LULLY, Jean-Baptiste (1632-1687). FRANCE. Born in Italy, Lully went to Paris at the age of 14 to work as a kitchen boy, but his musical talents were soon discovered. He was a violinist and dancer, but his real fame comes as the first composer of French opera.

MOZART, Wolfgang Amadeus (1756-1791). AUSTRIA. Mozart was a child prodigy, performing, composing and touring Europe at an early age. He worked as a composer and pianist, but died at a young age and in poverty. His musical genius is evident in his operas, symphonies, concertos, chamber music and piano sonatas.

NORTON, Christopher (born 1953). NEW ZEALAND. Norton is a teacher, composer and pianist. He moved to England in 1977 and wrote musicals, ballet scores, orchestral music and piano pieces. He composed the piano series *Microjazz* to help students understand and enjoy blues, jazz and rock styles.

PERDEW, Ruth (20th century). UNITED STATES. Perdew is a private piano teacher, clinician and composer in Denver, Colorado. Almost all of her pieces are educational piano solos and ensembles, often written to meet the needs of her own students.

*POOLE, Clifford (1916-2003). CANADA. Born in England, Poole came to Canada with his family at the age of nine. He and wife, Margaret Parsons, toured North America as a piano duo from 1954 to 1965. He taught at Western Ontario Conservatory, serving as its principal (1957-60), and later taught at The Royal Conservatory of Music in Toronto. Poole has had a distinguished careen in Toronto as a pianist, teacher, conductor, editor and composer. Some of his nine piano pieces appear under the pseudonyms of Charles Peerson, Ernest Marsen and J. Bach.

*PORTER, Beverly (born 1930). CANADA. Porter grew up in Vancouver, British Columbia, where she began her musical studies. She continued her studies at Queen's University in Kingston, Ontario where she now lives and teaches. Her piano pieces, written mostly for her own students, are both educational and entertaining.

PURCELL, Henry (1659-1695). BRITAIN. Purcell was perhaps the most gifted English composer of his time. He was trained as a chorister under John Blow at the Chapel Royal and later at Westminster Abbey, succeeding him as organist there. Purcell composed theatre music, church music, solo songs and instrumental music. He died at the early age of 36 and is buried in Westminster Abbey.

SCHEIN, Johann Hermann (1586-1630). GERMANY. As a child, Schein was a chorister in Dresden, Germany and later attended the University of Leipzig. He was well known as a teacher and composer in Germany and wrote church music, madrigals and suites. For many years, he held the post of cantor at St. Thomas Church in Leipzig, the same position J.S. Bach would hold 100 years later.

SCHMITT, Jacob (1803-1853). GERMANY. Schmitt was a pianist, composer and teacher. He came from a family of three generations of musicians. He composed many piano pieces in a Classical style and is most famous for his collections of sonatinas and sonatas.

SCHUBERT, Franz Peter (1797-1828). AUSTRIA. Schubert was a composer who learned violin from his father and piano from his older brother. Schubert enjoyed a large circle of devoted friends and patrons in Vienna, who often hosted evening musicales. These musicales were called 'Schubertiaden' because they performed only Schubert's music, usually with the composer at the piano. Though Schubert is perhaps most famous for his solo songs (called *Lieder* in German), he did compose instrumental music including some delightful pieces for piano.

SHOSTAKOVICH, Dmitri (1906-1975). RUSSIA. Born in St. Petersburg, Shostakovich's career was often hampered by the restrictions imposed on Soviet artists by the government. His music often has unexpected harmonies and rhythms. He composed the collection *Six Children's Pieces, Op. 69* in one day for his eight-year-old daughter, Gayla.

TAN, Chee-Hwa (born 1965). MALAYSIA. Chee-Hwa Tan received her musical training in the United States and has taught piano pedagogy at both the Oberlin Conservatory of Music and Southern Methodist University. She began composing piano pieces to encourage her own students to explore and express sound images at the piano, while at the same time developing their technique. Her works include *A Child's Garden of Verses* and *Circus Sonatinas*. Tan is also an associate editor for *Piano Life Magazine*.

TELEMANN, Georg Philipp (1681-1767). GERMANY. A composer and organist, Telemann was more famous during his lifetime than J.S. Bach. He was very active organizing and promoting concerts in Leipzig and later in Hamburg. His compositions included cantatas, passions, oratorios, operas, chamber music, harpsichord and organ music.

*TELFER, Nancy (born 1950). CANADA. A graduate of The University of Western Ontario, Telfer now lives in Sunderland, Ontario where she composes full-time. Her works for piano, voice, orchestra, chamber ensembles, and choirs have been performed and featured at festivals and conferences around the world. Many of her pieces are written with young performers in mind.

TÜRK, Daniel Gottlob (1756-1813). GERMANY. Türk was a composer, violinist and teacher. He was one of the first to write instructional pieces for children. His 160 piano pieces from *Pieces for Aspiring Players* have been compared to Schumann's *Album for the Young*.

WEBER, Carl Maria von (1786-1826). GERMANY. Weber is often considered the founder of German Romantic opera and is best known today as the composer of the opera *Der Freischütz* (the name means a marksman who uses magic bullets). He also composed some elegant piano pieces filled with beautiful melodies.